GREAT PRO SPORTS CHAMPIONSHIPS

GREAT NFL SUPER BOWL CHAMPIONSHIPS

by Ethan Olson

BrightPoint Press

San Diego, CA

BrightPoint Press

© 2024 BrightPoint Press
an imprint of ReferencePoint Press, Inc.
Printed in the United States

For more information, contact:
BrightPoint Press
PO Box 27779
San Diego, CA 92198
www.BrightPointPress.com

ALL RIGHTS RESERVED.

No part of this work covered by the copyright hereon may be reproduced or used in any form or by any means—graphic, electronic, or mechanical, including photocopying, recording, taping, web distribution, or information storage retrieval systems—without the written permission of the publisher.

LIBRARY OF CONGRESS CATALOGING-IN-PUBLICATION DATA

Names: Olson, Ethan, author.
Title: Great NFL Super Bowl championships / by Ethan Olson.
Other titles: Great National Football League Super Bowl championships
Description: San Diego, CA : BrightPoint Press, [2024] | Series: Great pro sports championships | Includes bibliographical references and index. | Audience: Ages 13 years | Audience: Grades 7-9
Identifiers: LCCN 2023009762 (print) | LCCN 2023009763 (eBook) | ISBN 9781678206604 (hardcover) | ISBN 9781678206611 (eBook)
Subjects: LCSH: Super Bowl--History--Juvenile literature. | Champions (Game)--Juvenile literature. | National Football League--History--Juvenile literature. | Football--United States--Juvenile literature.
Classification: LCC GV956.2.S8 O425 2024 (print) | LCC GV956.2.S8 (eBook) | DDC 796.332/6406--dc23/eng/20230308
LC record available at https://lccn.loc.gov/2023009762
LC eBook record available at https://lccn.loc.gov/2023009763

CONTENTS

AT A GLANCE   4

INTRODUCTION   6
SUPER SUNDAY

CHAPTER ONE   10
ELWAY ALL THE WAY

CHAPTER TWO   22
ONE MORE YARD

CHAPTER THREE   34
THE PERFECT UPSET

CHAPTER FOUR   46
DOWN, BUT NOT OUT

Glossary   58
Source Notes   59
For Further Research   60
Index   62
Image Credits   63
About the Author   64

AT A GLANCE

- The Super Bowl is one of the most beloved sporting events in the United States. It is the single most-watched sporting event on American television every year.

- Legendary quarterback John Elway of the Denver Broncos entered Super Bowl XXXII having already lost the big game three times in his career. But the fourth time proved a charm as the Broncos beat the Green Bay Packers in a thrilling finish.

- Not many expected a matchup between the Tennessee Titans and the St. Louis Rams in Super Bowl XXXIV. The two upstart teams combined for a great finish. The Rams held the Titans out of the end zone on the game's final play.

- The New England Patriots entered Super Bowl XLII with a perfect 18–0 record. However, the underdog New York Giants kept New England from a historic victory in a game filled with last-minute drama.

- The Patriots trailed the Atlanta Falcons 28–3 in the third quarter of Super Bowl LI. But led by superstar quarterback Tom Brady, New England rallied to win in the biggest comeback in Super Bowl history.

INTRODUCTION

SUPER SUNDAY

On February 5, 2017, Super Bowl LI was slipping away from the New England Patriots. The Atlanta Falcons were up 21–3 going into halftime. But New England wide receiver Julian Edelman was still confident. Edelman stood on the sidelines before the third quarter with legendary

New England quarterback Tom Brady. They both knew what it took to win a Super Bowl. Edelman had already won one. Brady had won four. As they waited

Julian Edelman makes a catch during Super Bowl LI.

for play to begin, Edelman leaned over to his quarterback.

"Let's go, baby," he said.[1] The star receiver then told Brady that when the Patriots came back to win, it would be a great story. And then they jogged onto the field to make history.

MOMENTS OF GREATNESS

Since 1967, the Super Bowl has provided many incredible stories. The **spectacle** includes pregame pageantry and halftime shows filled with pop stars. There are millions of fans watching around the world.

Military jets fly over the stadium before Super Bowl 50.

In the United States, the game is the most-watched sporting event on television each year. Many football fans consider Super Bowl Sunday to be a national holiday.

1
ELWAY ALL THE WAY

In the late 1980s, gunslinging quarterback John Elway led the Denver Broncos to three Super Bowls. But Denver had been blown out each time. It took until the 1997 season for Elway and the Broncos to get back to the big game.

The popular player was now thirty-seven years old. As he took the field in San Diego, California, for Super Bowl XXXII,

John Elway joined the Denver Broncos in 1983.

many Broncos fans could only wonder if this would be the great quarterback's last chance.

Winning wasn't going to be easy. The Broncos were up against the Green Bay Packers. The defending champions were led by one of the brightest stars in the National Football League (NFL). Green Bay quarterback Brett Favre had just won his third straight Most Valuable Player (MVP) Award.

The Packers offense went right to work after getting the ball first. Favre finished off a

Brett Favre threw for 256 yards and three touchdowns in Super Bowl XXXII.

quick drive with a 22-yard touchdown pass to star wide receiver Antonio Freeman.

The Broncos responded on their opening drive. All-Pro running back Terrell Davis powered in for a touchdown from one yard out. The game was tied at 7–7.

POWERING THROUGH

By the time the second quarter started, Davis was in pain. He was suffering from a **migraine** headache. But he was still on the field for the quarter's first play. With the ball at the Green Bay 1-yard line, Elway faked a handoff to Davis. The quarterback then took it in to make the score 14–7.

Soon after, Davis left the game. His vision was too blurry to play. He missed most of the second quarter recovering.

Broncos safety Steve Atwater forced a Favre fumble on the next drive. That set up the Broncos for a field goal to make it 17–7.

Safety Steve Atwater made the Pro Bowl eight times in ten seasons with the Broncos.

Since his touchdown pass in the first quarter, Favre had struggled. He had completed only one pass. He had an interception to go with his fumble. But with 7:38 left in the half, the superstar found his rhythm. He led the Packers on a seventeen-play drive that took all but twelve seconds off the clock. It ended when Favre hit tight end Mark Chmura on a six-yard touchdown pass.

THE HELICOPTER

Denver got the ball to start the second half. Davis was back in the game. But he fumbled on the first play. Green Bay quickly tied the game 17–17 with a field goal.

For years, Elway had been considered one of the league's toughest players. With 7:46 left in the third quarter, Denver took over at its own 8-yard line. In ten plays, Elway and Davis moved the Broncos to the

Terrell Davis (30) was named the Super Bowl's MVP after rushing for 157 yards and three touchdowns.

Green Bay 12-yard line. On third-and-six, Elway dropped back to pass. But no one was open. He took off running to the right side of the field.

As he got to the 5-yard line, three Green Bay defenders were waiting. Elway could have slid down on his backside. Defenders aren't allowed to hit a sliding quarterback. Instead, he leaped into the air. All three Packers slammed into him, sending Elway spinning. He landed hard at the 4-yard line. The "helicopter" play gave Denver a first down.

"You want to tell me the thirty-seven-year-old man doesn't want to win this game? That's sacrifice," said Broncos radio announcer Scott Hastings.[2] Two plays later, Davis scored to make it 24–17.

Elway goes airborne as he is hit by three Green Bay defenders.

FOR JOHN

The Packers took advantage of an Elway interception to tie the game early in the fourth quarter. It was still 24–24 with 3:50 left when Denver took over at the

Green Bay 49. Within two minutes the Broncos had moved to the Packers' 1-yard line.

Green Bay coach Mike Holmgren decided to let Davis score a touchdown. That way he could get the ball back with more time to tie the game. It was a big gamble. And it looked like it might work. The Packers moved the ball to the Denver 35 with 1:04 left. Then the Broncos' defense rose up. On fourth down, Denver linebacker John Mobley knocked away a pass intended for Chmura. Elway came back out to run out the clock. He finally had his title.

Broncos owner Pat Bowlen accepted the Vince Lombardi Trophy. He told the cheering crowd, "This one's for John."[3]

Elway led the Broncos to another win in Super Bowl XXXIII the next year. He then retired as one of the true legends of the game.

THIS ONE'S FOR PAT

The Broncos won the Super Bowl again after the 2015 season. John Elway was then the team's general manager. After the win, Elway told the crowd, "This one's for Pat." Pat Bowlen, the team's owner, had been suffering from Alzheimer's disease and was not with the team for the win.

Quoted in "18 Years Later, John Elway Declares 'This One's for Pat,'" *CBS News*, February 7, 2016. www.cbsnews.com.

2
ONE MORE YARD

In 1998, the St. Louis Rams finished 4–12. It was their ninth straight losing season. The 1999 season didn't look like it would be much better. Many experts picked the Rams to finish last in their division. That was before starting quarterback

Trent Green was injured for the year in a preseason game.

In his place, Rams coach Dick Vermeil turned to unknown twenty-seven-year-old Kurt Warner. No NFL teams had wanted him out of college. Warner worked in a

Kurt Warner jogs onto the field during Super Bowl XXXIV.

grocery store and played arena football while waiting for an NFL chance. Now given one, Warner became an instant star. He threw 41 touchdown passes and won MVP. The Rams also had star running back Marshall Faulk. The twenty-six-year-old became the second running back to gain 1,000 yards both rushing and receiving.

The Rams piled up points and finished 13–3. Along the way their high-scoring offense became known as "the Greatest Show on Turf." St. Louis then beat the Minnesota Vikings and Tampa Bay Buccaneers in the playoffs. They were off to

Super Bowl XXXIV at the Georgia Dome in Atlanta, Georgia.

The Tennessee Titans hadn't made the playoffs since 1993, when they were still the Houston Oilers. But behind powerful running back Eddie George and gutsy quarterback Steve McNair, they also finished 13–3. A tough defense kept

ON THE MOVE

Both teams playing in Super Bowl XXXIV had just changed cities. The Tennessee Titans had been the Houston Oilers until the 1997 season. The St. Louis Rams had moved from Los Angeles in 1995. The Rams stayed in St. Louis until 2015. That year, they moved back to Los Angeles.

Tennessee Titans running back Eddie George ran for 1,304 yards and nine touchdowns during the 1999 season.

Tennessee in most games. Rookie defender Jevon Kearse had 14.5 **sacks**. His athletic moves earned him the nickname "the Freak."

DEFENSIVE STANDS

Leading up to the Super Bowl, experts wondered if the Rams could be stopped. But the Titans held their own. St. Louis put up 294 yards of offense in the first half. But the Rams couldn't get into the end zone. Instead, they scored nine points on field goals by kicker Jeff Wilkins.

However, Tennessee's offense was shut down completely. The Rams held the Titans to 89 yards and no points. St. Louis took a 9–0 lead into halftime.

Tennessee finally got a drive going early in the second half. But kicker Al Del Greco's

47-yard attempt was blocked. The Rams then marched down the field. They scored on a Warner nine-yard touchdown pass to Torry Holt.

Down 16–0, the Titans started to climb back. McNair and George led a twelve-play, 66-yard drive. George slammed in from the 1-yard line to make it 16–6. But the Titans' **two-point conversion** didn't work.

After a quick defensive stop, the Titans took over at their 21-yard line. The 6-foot-3, 235-pound George then carried the ball eight times on a thirteen-play drive. He finished it off with a two-yard touchdown.

Rams receivers Torry Holt (left) and Isaac Bruce (right) celebrate after Holt's touchdown catch in the third quarter.

After Del Greco's extra point, St. Louis was up 16–13 with 7:53 left.

Once again, Tennessee's defense stopped the Rams quickly. With 3:08 left, Del Greco completed the comeback. A 43-yard field goal made it 16–16.

All season long, the Rams had burned opponents with their long touchdown passes. On the first play of the next drive, Warner dropped back and lobbed a pass to the right sideline. Receiver Isaac Bruce caught it in full stride and raced to the end zone. The 73-yard pass put the Rams back on top 23–16 with just over two minutes left.

THE LONGEST YARD

A holding penalty on the kickoff pushed the Titans back to their own 12. McNair led another long drive. With 22 seconds left the Titans faced third-and-five at the Rams'

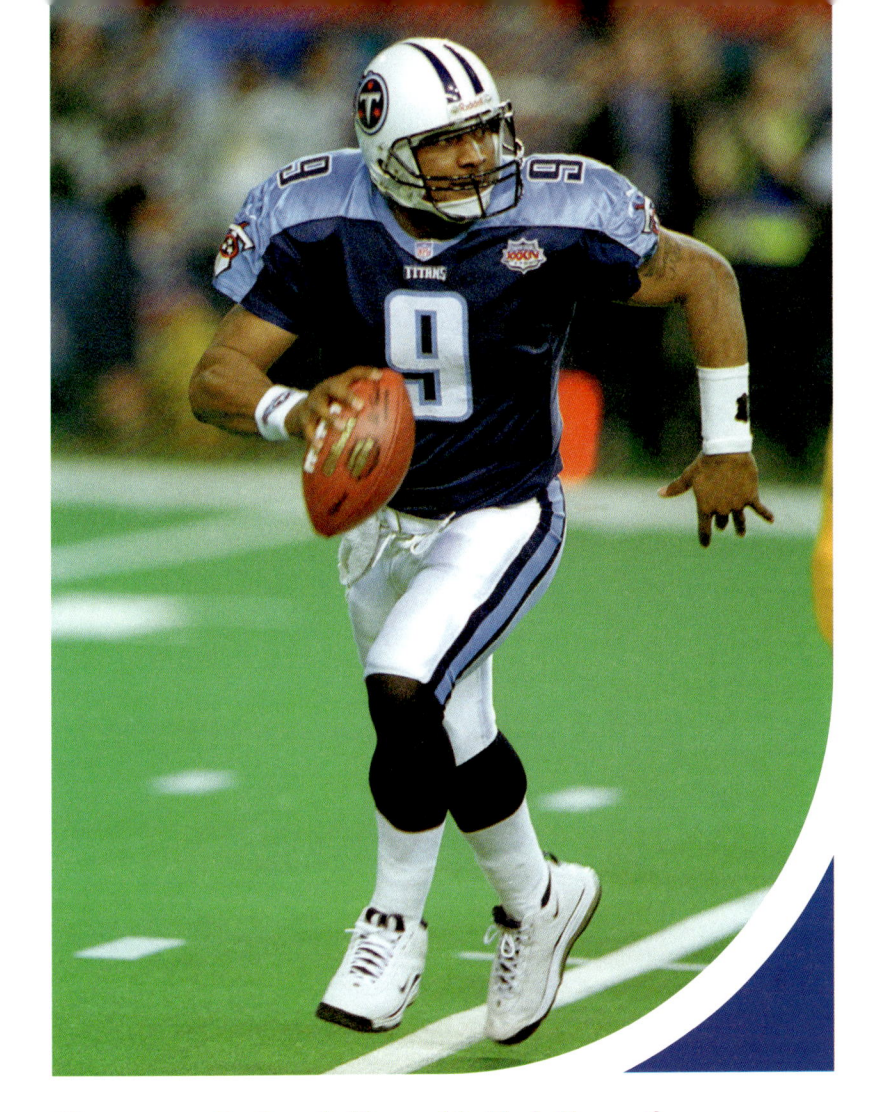

Titans quarterback Steve McNair threw for 214 yards in Super Bowl XXXIV.

26-yard line. McNair scrambled away from two sack attempts, then hit receiver Kevin Dyson at the 10.

McNair's escape had taken seventeen seconds off the clock. After a time-out, the Titans had time for only one more play. Dyson cut across the middle of the field. He caught McNair's pass at the 5-yard line. Rams linebacker Mike Jones quickly wrapped Dyson up. Dyson stretched the ball out, desperate to reach the goal line. Jones squeezed him tight, using all of his strength to drag the receiver down. Dyson was just short of the end zone. The game was over.

"I knew the only way he was getting in was if I missed the tackle, and I wasn't

Tennessee's Kevin Dyson (87) is tackled by Rams linebacker Mike Jones on the game's final play.

missing any tackle," Jones said, reflecting on the moment.[4]

"The Tackle" kept the Titans from completing the comeback. The Rams' offense had set many records during the year. But it was their defense that won the game in a Super Bowl that came down to the last yard.

3
THE PERFECT UPSET

By the start of the 2007 season, the New England Patriots were the NFL's most dominant team. They had won three Super Bowls since 2000. And during the 2007 season, the Patriots looked unbeatable.

In the last game of the season, the Patriots beat the New York Giants 38–35.

New England star quarterback Tom Brady threw his record fiftieth touchdown pass. Receiver Randy Moss caught twenty-three of them to set another record.

Eli Manning (10) and the New York Giants were heavy underdogs against Tom Brady (12) and the New England Patriots in Super Bowl XLII.

The win also capped a perfect 16–0 regular season for New England. The Patriots seemed sure to be in the Super Bowl. And most football fans thought they were certain to win.

Meanwhile, that 38–35 loss dropped the Giants to 10–6. They made the playoffs, but as a wild-card team. Coach Tom Coughlin's team won three close **postseason** games.

THE PERFECT SEASON

Only one team has ever finished an NFL season with a perfect record. The 1972 Miami Dolphins finished the then fourteen-game regular season perfect. They then won two playoff games before beating Washington in Super Bowl VII to finish 17–0.

That sent New York into Super Bowl XLII in Glendale, Arizona. The Patriots, as expected, were waiting.

THE SLUGFEST

One way to stop the Patriots' offense was to keep it off the field. The Giants got the ball first and did just that. New York's opening drive lasted sixteen plays. Unfortunately, it didn't get the Giants into the end zone. The Giants settled for a field goal from kicker Lawrence Tynes.

Brady and the Patriots quickly answered. Running back Laurence Maroney scored a touchdown on the first play of the second quarter. It was 7–3 New England.

It stayed that way for a while. The Giants struggled to move the ball. New England was having more success. But key New York defensive plays stopped the Patriots.

STEPPING UP

It was still 7–3 when the fourth quarter started. New York took over at its own 20-yard line. The Giants were led by fourth-year quarterback Eli Manning. Many New York fans wondered if he was good enough. That season he had led the NFL

New York's Justin Tuck (91) strips the ball from Brady in the second quarter.

with twenty interceptions. But Manning immediately threw a 45-yard pass. Five plays later the quarterback tossed a five-yard touchdown pass to little-used wide receiver David Tyree. Suddenly, New York led 10–7.

Brady had faced pressure from New York's excellent defensive line all game. Led by Michael Strahan, the Giants had sacked Brady four times through the game's first three quarters.

Still, the Patriots had a chance to win. Brady and the offense took over with 7:54 left and started chewing up yards. Starting at its own 20, New England went 80 yards in 5:12. On third-and-goal from the Giants' 6-yard line, Brady lobbed a go-ahead touchdown to Moss.

Randy Moss catches a fourth-quarter touchdown pass to put New England ahead in Super Bowl XLII.

UNSUNG HERO

Before the Giants got the ball back, Strahan tried to inspire his offense on the sideline.

"17–14, fellas. One touchdown, we are world

champions. Believe it, and it will happen," he said.[5]

With just over one minute remaining, the Giants faced third-and-five at their own 44. As Manning dropped back, he was swarmed by New England pass rushers. Even though some had a hold of his jersey, Manning escaped. He then hurled a desperate pass down the middle of the field.

Waiting for it was Tyree. The receiver had caught only four passes in the regular season. He leaped in the air. So did Patriots safety Rodney Harrison. As Tyree came

David Tyree (85) squeezes the ball to his helmet as New England safety Rodney Harrison tries to knock it away.

down with the ball, Harrison tried to punch it away. Tyree held on by pinning the ball to his helmet as he hit the turf.

The incredible play became known as the "helmet catch." Before that moment, few football fans knew who Tyree was. The play made him an instant Super Bowl legend.

Four plays later, Manning hit receiver Plaxico Burress to make it 17–14. There were 29 seconds left when the Patriots took over. Another sack eventually forced New England into a fourth-and-twenty play at its own 16. Brady's desperation pass for Moss fell incomplete. The perfect season was over.

Manning's two fourth-quarter touchdown passes earned him the MVP Award.

Manning celebrates the Giants' victory in Super Bowl XLII.

However, it was Tyree's miracle catch that fans remembered for years to come. It set the stage for the Giants to finish off perhaps the greatest Super Bowl **upset** of all time.

4

DOWN, BUT NOT OUT

Quarterback Tom Brady and coach Bill Belichick first teamed up for the New England Patriots in 2000. By the 2016 season, the pair had been to six Super Bowls. They had won four. There wasn't much left for the dominant Patriots to achieve. But in Super Bowl LI in

Houston, Texas, New England pulled one more surprise.

The Patriots had scored 441 points that season. Yet their opponents, the Atlanta Falcons, reached the Super Bowl with an even better offense. Dan Quinn's

Quarterback Tom Brady (left) and head coach Bill Belichick (right) helped turn the New England Patriots into a dynasty in the 2000s.

team scored 540 points during an 11–5 regular season. The team was led by MVP quarterback Matt Ryan. Most fans thought Super Bowl LI would be an offensive game.

SOARING FALCONS

Surprisingly, neither team scored in the first quarter. The Falcons took off in the second. Two quick touchdowns put Atlanta up 14–0 with 8:48 left in the half.

Brady looked like he was settling in on the next drive. Over six minutes, he led New England to the Atlanta 23. Then Brady tried to sneak a pass over the middle to receiver

Falcons cornerback Robert Alford celebrates his 82-yard interception return in the second quarter.

Danny Amendola. Falcons cornerback Robert Alford jumped in for an interception. Alford sprinted 82 yards to make it 21–0.

A late first-half field goal got New England on the board. But no team had ever come

BIGGEST SUPER BOWL COMEBACKS

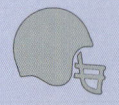

Super Bowl LI—New England 34, Atlanta 28 (OT)
New England trailed 28–3

Super Bowl LVII—Kansas City 38, Philadelphia 35
Kansas City trailed 24–14

Super Bowl LIV—Kansas City 31, San Francisco 20
Kansas City trailed 20–10

Super Bowl XLIX—New England 28, Seattle 24
New England trailed 24–14

Super Bowl XLIV—New Orleans 31, Indianapolis 17
New Orleans trailed 10–0

Super Bowl XXII—Washington 42, Denver 10
Washington trailed 10–0

Source: "Biggest Comebacks in Super Bowl History, From Chiefs' Rally Against 49ers to Patriots' Legendary '28–3,'" Sporting News, 2020. www.sportingnews.com.

New England's comeback in Super Bowl LI was the largest in the game's history.

from so far behind to win a Super Bowl. And it got even worse early in the second half. Ryan led an 85-yard drive to make it 28–3 with 8:31 left in the third quarter.

HERE WE GO

Early in the third quarter, Brady and receiver Julian Edelman had stood on the sideline pumping each other up. Now they had to turn it on between the sidelines. "Let's go. We gotta play harder! We gotta play tougher! Everything we got!" Brady demanded of his teammates.[6]

On the next drive, the Patriots marched 75 yards. Running back James White caught a five-yard touchdown pass. Kicker Steven Gostkowski missed the extra point. Atlanta was still in control. The Falcons were leading 28–9.

Suddenly, the game flipped. The Patriots quickly got the ball back. Another long drive ended with a Gostkowski field goal. It was 28–12 with 9:44 left in the game.

The Patriots' defense then made a big play. Linebacker Donta'a Hightower blitzed and sacked Ryan. The Falcons quarterback fumbled. It was recovered by defensive tackle Alan Branch. Five plays later, Brady

TOM THE LEGEND

Tom Brady left the Patriots after the 2019 season. He had won six Super Bowls with the team. Brady added one more with the Tampa Bay Buccaneers after the 2020 season. He retired in 2023 with more Super Bowl wins than any other player.

hit Amendola for a six-yard score. A two-point conversion made it 28–20.

The Patriots got the ball back with 3:30 left. The problem was, they were at their own 9-yard line. Two **completions** moved them up to the 36. Brady then threw a pass down the middle, looking for Edelman. Alford got two hands on it, knocking it up in the air. Edelman dived after the tipped ball with two other Atlanta defenders.

After a short delay, the referees said Edelman had somehow caught it. The Falcons challenged the ruling. Replays showed Edelman had indeed made an incredible grab. He had plucked it from inches off the ground. Even after a slight bobble, Edelman held on without the ball hitting the turf. "It was probably about 80 percent luck, to tell the truth," Edelman said later.[7]

Edelman's miracle catch set up White for a one-yard touchdown run with 57 seconds left. Brady converted the two-point play to Amendola. For the first time ever, the Super Bowl would go to overtime.

The Patriots won the coin toss. They quickly went to work on the stunned Falcons defense. Brady completed passes

Julian Edelman (11) reaches to secure the ball just before it hits the turf in the fourth quarter.

to four different receivers on the drive. Finally, a pass interference penalty on Atlanta linebacker De'Vondre Campbell set New England up with first-and-goal at the Atlanta 2-yard line.

Brady tried a pass on first down. It was nearly intercepted in the end zone. On second down, Brady gave the ball to White. Falcons safety Ricardo Allen met White at the line of scrimmage. But the Patriots running back dragged him into the end zone. The Patriots comeback was complete. The final score was 34–28.

Mathematical models had given the Falcons a 99.8 percent chance to win when they were up 28–3. But the Patriots had never stopped believing they could come back. In Atlanta, "28–3" became a hard score to hear. But in New England,

New England running back James White scores the game-winning touchdown in overtime.

it was another piece of the Patriots'

incredible **legacy**.

GLOSSARY

completions

forward passes that are caught before the ball touches the ground

legacy

the lasting impact of an event or someone's actions

migraine

a headache that causes throbbing pain usually on one side of the head

postseason

another term for playoffs

sacks

times when the quarterback is tackled behind the line of scrimmage while attempting to pass

spectacle

a memorable event

two-point conversion

an option to get two points by getting the ball into the end zone after a touchdown, instead of kicking a single extra point

upset

a victory by a team that is not expected to win

SOURCE NOTES

INTRODUCTION: SUPER SUNDAY

1. Quoted in Will Brinson, "Julian Edelman Predicted the Patriots' Super Bowl Comeback at Halftime," *CBS Sports*, February 8, 2017. www.cbssports.com.

CHAPTER ONE: ELWAY ALL THE WAY

2. Quoted in "#8 Elway's Helicopter | NFL | Top 10 Super Bowl Plays," *YouTube*, uploaded by NFL, October 26, 2015. www.youtube.com.

3. Quoted in Jeff Legwald, "Pat Bowlen: 'This One's for John' Highlighted a Hall of Fame Career," *ESPN*, July 31, 2019. www.espn.com.

CHAPTER TWO: ONE MORE YARD

4. Quoted in Ray Ratto, "The Most Super of Stops," *ESPN*, n.d. www.espn.com.

CHAPTER THREE: THE PERFECT UPSET

5. Quoted in Dan Salomone, "One Giant Victory: An Oral History of the Winning Drive in Super Bowl XLII," *New York Giants*, February 9, 2023. www.giants.com.

CHAPTER FOUR: DOWN, BUT NOT OUT

6. Quoted in Doug Kyed, "Best Lines from Patriots, Falcons on 'Inside the NFL: Super Bowl LI'," *NESN*, February 8, 2017. www.nesn.com.

7. Quoted in Daniel Mano, "Julian Edelman Shares Patriots' Halftime Speech Before Historic Comeback," *San Jose Mercury News*, February 9, 2017. www.mercurynews.com.

FOR FURTHER RESEARCH

BOOKS

Will Graves, *GOATs of Football*. Minneapolis, MN: Abdo Publishing, 2022.

David Halprin, *Football Biographies for Kids: The Greatest NFL Players from the 1960s to Today*. Emeryville, CA: Rockridge Press, 2022.

Barry Wilner, *The Greatest NFL Coaches of All Time*. San Diego, CA: BrightPoint Press, 2021.

INTERNET SOURCES

Judy Battista, "Giants Stun Patriots in Super Bowl XLII," *New York Times*, February 4, 2008. www.nytimes.com.

Greg Bishop, "Suspended Disbelief: Tom Brady Seals Status as Greatest QB Ever in Super Bowl LI," *Sports Illustrated*, February 7, 2017. www.si.com.

Richard Justice, "Elway, AFC Finally Have Super Moment," *Washington Post*, January 26, 1998. www.washingtonpost.com.

TSN Archives, "Kevin Dyson, Mike Jones Meet Again to Discuss 'The Tackle' In Titans-Rams Super Bowl," *Sporting News*, February 13, 2021. www.sportingnews.com.

WEBSITES

National Football League
www.nfl.com

NFL.com is the National Football League's official website. It contains league news and information as well as individual pages for all thirty-two NFL franchises.

Pro Football Reference
www.pro-football-reference.com

Pro Football Reference is a research website that offers accurate statistical data for every game and player ever associated with the National Football League.

Pro Football Hall of Fame
www.profootballhof.com

The Pro Football Hall of Fame's website contains information about the Hall's members as well as the sport's history.

INDEX

Alford, Robert, 49, 53
Allen, Ricardo, 56
Amendola, Danny, 49, 53–54
Atwater, Steve, 14

Belichick, Bill, 46
Bowlen, Pat, 21
Brady, Tom, 7–8, 35, 37, 40, 44, 46, 48, 51–56
Branch, Alan, 52
Bruce, Isaac, 30
Burress, Plaxico, 44

Campbell, De'Vondre, 55
Chmura, Mark, 16, 20
Coughlin, Tom, 36

Davis, Terrell, 13–14, 16, 18, 20
Del Greco, Al, 27, 29
Dyson, Kevin, 31–32

Edelman, Julian, 6–8, 51, 53–54
Elway, John, 10, 14, 16–21

Faulk, Marshall, 24
Favre, Brett, 12, 14–16
Freeman, Antonio, 13

George, Eddie, 25, 28
Gostkowski, Stephen, 51–52
Green, Trent, 23

Harrison, Rodney, 42–43
Hastings, Scott, 18
Hightower, Donta'a, 52
Holmgren, Mike, 20
Holt, Torry, 28

Jones, Mike, 32–33

Kearse, Jevon, 26

Manning, Eli, 38–39, 42, 44
Maroney, Laurence, 37
McNair, Steve, 25, 28, 30–32
Mobley, John, 20
Moss, Randy, 35, 40, 44

Quinn, Dan, 47

Ryan, Matt, 48, 50, 52

Strahan, Michael, 40–41

Tynes, Lawrence, 37
Tyree, David, 40, 42–45

Vermeil, Dick, 23

Warner, Kurt, 23–24, 28, 30
White, James, 51, 54, 56
Wilkins, Jeff, 27

IMAGE CREDITS

Cover: © Jim Mahoney/AP Images
5: © Lev Radin/Shutterstock Images
7: © Ben Liebenberg/AP Images
9: © Spc. Brandon C. Dyer/US Department of Defense
11: © Paul Spinelli/AP Images
13: © Paul Spinelli/AP Images
15: © Paul Spinelli/AP Images
17: © Lenny Ignelzi/AP Images
19: © Elaine Thompson/AP Images
23: © Tom DiPace/AP Images
26: © Al Messerschmidt/AP Images
29: © Paul Spinelli/AP Images
31: © Kevin Reece/AP Images
33: © Kevin Terrell/AP Images
35: © David J. Phillip/AP Images
39: © Chris O'Meara/AP Images
41: © Gene Puskar/AP Images
43: © Gene Puskar/AP Images
45: © Ben Liebenberg/AP Images
47: © Tom Strattman/AP Images
49: © Damian Strohmeyer/AP Images
50: © Red Line Editorial
55: © Patrick Semansky/AP Images
57: © Charlie Riedel/AP Images

ABOUT THE AUTHOR

Ethan Olson is a sportswriter and editor based in Minneapolis.